Easy Dorm RECIPES

Christine McGivern

Culinary Artist Creative Developer

Great On-The-Go Recipes for College Dorm and Sophisticated, After-Schoolkids

Easy Pasta Dishes

Fulton Books
Meadville, PA

Published by Fulton Books 2023

ISBN 979-8-88982-092-5 (paperback)
ISBN 979-8-88982-093-2 (digital)

Printed in the United States of America

Contents

Author's Note

To the fellow dormer or sophisticated kid,

To survive on your own, one must adapt to the habitual living you are dealt. Adapt to your tools and space and create with what surrounds you, with note to rules of cleanliness and hygiene principles.

This book of recipes gives you a few simple methods to create a few fun, easy, and tasty meals with convenience. You may have some common items to stock your cabinets, such as ketchup, salt, pepper, bottled water, and noodle varieties; you can keep them on hand to use at your convenience. You are also open to create with noodle choices and seasonings to your liking.

This book will help the dormer, who may have limited time and space, to enjoy a good, unconventional pasta dish, as well as help the sophisticated kid on their way to culinary creation with little supervision after school with these easy methods.

Become a ghetto chef superstar.

> Ghetto superstar
> That is what you are
> Reaching for the stars
> Come away with me…
> We can rely on each other. ("Ghetto Supastar
> [That Is What You Are]," Pras)

Introduction

WHAT YOU'LL NEED ESSENTIALS: microwave, oven mitts, microwavable safe bowl with lid, water, pasta, and great dishes explored. You may have a variety of items lying around in your pantry, which you may not realize can be combined for a great dish creation. This book will give you a few easy recipes to try for your dorm or after-school life on your own.

Safety Tip: Be careful with bowl from the microwave, always use oven mitts, and keep hands steady so that water does not drip from the bowl. It will be very hot. In case of accidental burn to skin, run burn under cool/cold water.

Tip: Have your ingredients out ahead of time, clean up immediately after (including any spills in the microwave), dispose garbage, rinse bowls and utensils. Handy items that may be helpful: napkins, paper towels, and plates.

Keep in mind that some microwaves heat differently; if unsure of your microwave strength, heat in half increments and check the dish until you're comfortable with your cooking times for later use. Record times for your own microwave in your notes section.

Most dishes are single-serving, so you don't have to eat what your roommate eats. If serving two, use a larger bowl, permitted it fits in your microwave, and multiply ingredients by two. Otherwise, you can create and compare dishes with your friend or roommate. A friendly contest may be a fun way to break the ice on a first day in the dorm or just to have fun during a boring downtime.

Important: Always wash your hands before the start of cooking. It is also good to wash your hands after your meal, as well.

Sweet Almond Pasta Swirl

Ingredients:
- rotelle pasta
- lightly salted almonds
- salt
- pepper
- 1/2 to 1 tbsp of butter or sub olive oil
- sweet seasoning
- bottled or tap water

In a microwavable safe bowl (with cover), add pasta and cover with water. Heat for 5 to 7 minutes up to 10 minutes depending on strength of the microwave or until pasta becomes al dente, then toss pasta with fork (there should still be a bit of water left, if not, add a tiny bit more). Add almonds, salt, pepper, butter, and sweet seasoning. Continue cooking for 2 minutes until butter is melted and pasta and almonds are fully cooked. Note that almonds will be slightly softened but can keep crisp texture. Once complete, there may be a light glaze of butter sauce. Toss to cover noodles and add additional seasoning to taste, if desired.

Note: If you are using olive oil, wait till pasta are almost fully cooked, then you can add salt and pepper with water and cook for an additional 1 minute for pasta to soften. Add seasoning and olive oil, then toss and cook for a minute.

Nondairy Sweet Chilli Mac (Chester Cheetos-Flavored)

Ingredients:
    choice of pasta
    bottled or tap water
    salt
    pepper
    ketchup
    chilli seasoning
    Cheetos cheese
    sweet seasoning
    penne pasta (picture below)

In a microwavable safe bowl (with cover), add pasta and cover with water. Heat for 5 to 7minutes up to 10 minutes depending on strength of the microwave. Cook till al dente (a very little bit of water should be left), then toss lightly with fork. Add salt, pepper, ketchup (four packets), a heavy dash of chilli seasoning, and about 2 tbsp of Chester Cheeto Cheese (artificial). Continue cooking for 1 to 2 minutes more until pasta softens.

Note: The blend of remaining water, ketchup, and seasoning create this light tasty sauce for your pasta. Add additional seasoning to taste if desired.

Healthy Carrot-Apple Pasta Swirl

Ingredients:
  rotelle pasta
  bottled or tap water
  salt
  pepper
  carrot-apple puree

Healthy Carrot-Apple Pasta Swirl Twist—
Coconut Infused

Sub cavatappi noodles for rotelle. Use
tropical coconut water, add sweet seasoning,
and follow other directions as described.

Healthy Spinach-Apple Pasta Swirl

Ingredients:
    rotelle pasta
    bottled or tap water
    salt
    pepper
    3 oz spinach-apple puree

Healthy Spinach-Apple Pasta Swirl Twist—Coconut Infused with Spicy Dill Pickle Almonds

Sub cavatappi noodles for rotelle. Use coconut water, add half of the single-packed spicy dill pickle almonds (21.5 g), then follow other directions as directed.

In a microwavable safe bowl, cover pasta with water. Heat for 5 to 7 minutes or up to 10 minutes depending on strength of the microwave until al dente. Toss lightly with fork. A small amount of water should still be remaining. Add in salt, pepper, and carrot-apple or spinach-apple puree. Continue cooking until pasta is fully cooked for about 2 minutes. To avoid overboiling with puree, heat for 1 minute, then toss lightly with fork and heat for an additional minute. When finished, you will have a light carrot-apple sauce or spinach-apple variation. Add additional seasoning to taste if desired (recommended: sweet seasoning). Almonds can also be added to this dish as directed in "Sweet Almond Pasta Swirl" recipe.

Note: To thicken, let stand in microwave for a minute to cool, stir, and heat for an additional 45 seconds. You can also add butter to thicken as well. If too thick, add water; however, a touch more seasoning may be required as well to taste.

Hint: You can also try infusing your pasta with cucumber water. This would especially go well with a cold pasta salad dish. See "Types of Pasta" note.

Simple Buttered Pasta

Ingredients:
    choice of pasta
    ½ to 1 tbsp butter
    salt
    pepper
    bottled or tap water
    other ingredients to taste if desired are basil and thyme

<table>
<tr>
<td>Cook for 10 minutes for thin spaghetti or thicker pastas. Stir halfway through. And cook for an additional 2 minutes after seasoning.</td>
<td></td>
<td>Note: When using spaghetti, a microwave-safe square or rectangle bowl may be required to fully cover pasta with water more easily. Otherwise, break stems into smaller pieces and make sure water completely covers the stems.</td>
</tr>
</table>

In a microwavable safe bowl, cover pasta with water. Heat for 5 to 7 minutes or up to 10 minutes depending on strength of the microwave or until al dente. Toss noodles lightly with fork. Add seasoning (salt and pepper) and butter, then toss and cook for additional 1 to 2 minutes till pasta softens and butter is melted.

Note: When using spaghetti, a microwave safe square or rectangle bowl may be required to fully cover pasta with water more easily. Otherwise, break stems into smaller pieces and make sure water completely covers stems.

Cook for 10 minutes for thin spaghetti or thicker pastas. Stir halfway through and cook for an additional 2 minutes after seasoning.

Simple Pasta with Olive Oil Twist

Sub olive oil about 1 to 3 tsp in place of butter.

Ziti Rigati with Olive Oil

Simple 'n' Crazy Ketchup Twist

Sub or add in ketchup with your selection of pasta.

Cavatappi Noodles with Sweet Seasoning and Ketchup Twist

Longevity Tao Noodles

Ingredients:

long noodles (or packaged Ramen noodles, keep seasoning to side for later recipe)

In a microwavable safe bowl, cover noodles with water. Heat for 5 to 7 minutes or up to 10 minutes depending on strength of the microwave or until al dente or tender.

The noodle way of life has been around for ages BC. The *Tao* translates, simplified, to the *way of life*. How you live, sleep, and eat determine a part of who you are. The individual is unyieldingly unwielding, meaning greatly complex in their own. With the variations of ancestry in today's world, the taste bud of one to another may undoubtedly be different. You can, with a blank slate, create about anything; these noodles of longevity are to an unyielding, unwielding art in that you can create with it what you may or you may choose to eat them just the way they are.

General Tso
Longevity
Tao Noodles

Homestyled Chicken Noodle Noods

Ingredients:

    cavatappi noodles
    bottled or tap water
    salt
    pepper
    chicken flavor/seasoning

Hint: You can put your Ramen noodles to the side for later use and use the chicken flavor or keep chicken seasoning on hand in your cabinet space. Add on your choice of cooked meat or vegetables to homestyle your own.

In a microwavable safe bowl with cover, heat for 5 to 7 minutes up to 10 minutes or until noodles are al dente, then toss in salt, pepper, and seasoning. Heat for an additional 1 to 2 minutes.

Add a touch of your own style with your favorite cooked meat or veggies to top your noods.

See the next page for a flavorful BBQ side dish for your next summer or game party.

Brown Sugar Sweet BBQ Chilli Homestyled Noods

Ingredients:
    homestyled noods
    sweet brown sugar BBQ sauce
    chilli seasoning
    sweet seasoning

With your homestyled noods (cooked as directed on the previous page), add 4 tbsp of sweet brown sugar BBQ sauce, chilli seasoning, and sweet seasoning. Toss lightly with fork covering noodles with a light coating of the sauce. Heat for an additional 1 to 2 minutes. Toss again lightly and enjoy.

Suggestion: Add red and green peppers or real hamburger chilli to serve as side dish at your next BBQ.

Healthy Corn Star Chicken BBQ Bowl

This is a great dish for kids to enjoy. Look for more kid- or baby-friendly dishes in Easy Kid/Baby Meals.

Ingredients:
  baby star pastina
  giant green corn
  salt
  pepper
  1/2 packet or about 1 1/2 tsp chicken seasoning
  1 to 2 tbsp of sweet or regular BBQ sauce
  Add small diced grilled chicken if desired or sub other vegetable variety favorite. Mixed veg is recommended.

In a microwavable safe bowl, add ingredients and toss lightly to mix evenly. Heat for 3 to 5 minutes depending on strength of the microwave. Lightly toss with fork to stir in BBQ sauce.

Pastina cooks very quickly and needs less time to fully cook. The liquid with corn is all that is needed to cook your pastina. You can also add water to make a pastina soup depending on you or your kids' preference. Small precooked diced chicken can also be added to add protein to your dish. No more than 2 tenders diced for 1 small single serving. One can or bag of corn can make 2 to 3 servings. If using frozen corn, heat first until thawed and warm, then add other ingredients as directed.

This may be a great bread bowl filling.

Taco Shell Pasta

Ingredients:
    shell pasta
    bottled or tap water
    salt
    pepper
    taco seasoning

Note: You can add real taco shell or tortilla crumbles on top and your favorite taco fixings if desired (lettuce, shredded cheese, etc.). Also try a gordita shell stuffed with Taco Shell Pasta (add melted shredded cheese if desired) for a taco Mac Grilled Cheese Gordita. Chicken, ground beef, or other meat can also be added if you have precooked on hand (see appendix A). Look for a more in-depth version in a later edition. This is intended for a quick, tasty convenience.

Variation:

Chester Cheeto Nondairy Taco Elbow Mac with Salsa and Sour Cream Topped with a Taco Mac Taco

Sub elbow mac for shell pasta. Add Chester Cheeto (artificial cheese flavor seasoning).

Cheesy without the cheese.

In a microwavable safe bowl, cover noodles with water. Heat for 5 to 7 minutes or up to 10 minutes depending on strength of the microwave or until al dente. Add in salt, pepper, and taco seasoning. Toss lightly and heat for an additional 1 to 2 minutes. Enjoy your tasty taco shells or see note above and decide what you can add to give your shells a crunch or top things up.

Stuffed Taco Shells
(Contains Dairy)

Ingredients:
4 to 7 large shells
bottled or tap water
salt
pepper
taco seasoning
salsa (medium or hot, individual-sized servings work best for one dish)

Filling:
1 to 4 oz sour cream
1 to 2 tsp taco seasoning top with salsa and shredded cheese (if desired)

Note: Dairy items must be stored in a mini fridge until ready to use. Refrigerate salsa and other perishable items such as sour cream and shredded cheese after opening.

In a microwavable safe bowl, cover noodles with water. Heat for 5 to 7 minutes or up to 12 minutes depending on strength of the microwave or until al dente. Toss noodles in taco seasoning and heat for 1 minute. Use a plate and spoon in mixing sour cream and taco seasoning. Top with salsa and shredded cheese. Heat for additional 1 to 2 minutes or if you have a toaster oven, place on toaster oven-safe serving dish and bake until cheese is melted. If using toaster oven method, make sure noodles are fully cooked. You can add filling to fully cooked noodles if baking.

Simple Pasta with Tomato Sauce

Ingredients:
    simple buttered pasta or pasta with olive oil
    choice of jarred or canned tomato sauce
    add basil or another Italian herb if desired

Note: These recipes are for quick, convenient microwavable dishes, which is why canned or jarred sauce is used. Look for other additions or instructions on homemade tomato sauce.

Heat pasta as directed in Simple Buttered Pasta or pasta with olive oil. Add 3 to 4 tablespoons of jarred or canned sauce with seasoning butter or olive oil and continue by heating for additional 1 to 2 minutes.

Note: Remaining canned sauce must be stored in separate container and refrigerated after opening. Jarred sauce can be closed tightly and stored in refrigerator for later use.

Reader's Notes

As an emerging chef, you may want to jot down noteworthy ideas, measurements, times, etc.

Glossary of Terms

adapt. To become accustomed to; get used to.

al dente. Noodle cooked thoroughly yet still slightly firm.

blanched. With vegetables, drop and submerge in boiling water to sanitize and soften slightly.

boil. Heating to a temperature that cooks thoroughly.

create. To invent or make.

creation. Something that was made or invented.

convenience. On hand; practical; at one's means of use.

cover ingredients. Referring to water for recipe; water covers noodles completely.

culinary. The art/style of cooking, creating meals and dishes.

dorm. A room where a college student stays in while attending school.

dormer. A person who stays in a dorm room.

dripage. Dripping of unwanted juices.

essentials. Things that will definitely be needed.

habitual. Style of living; referring to habitat.

hygiene. One's own cleanliness.

increments. Segments; short periods of time.

infused. To add inside something or in the center of (e.g., coconut flavor infused with the noodles).

liking. Preference; what you like.

limited. Having only a few; not many on hand; referring to a short period of time.

methods. The way you go about something.

microwave. Electronic device that heats food to temperatures based on time.

microwavable safe bowl. Nonmetal bowl designed to withstand heat of microwave without melting.

overboil. Boiling that goes over the edge of container, bowl, or dish.
principals. Guide or standards.
seasoning. A blend of spices and/or herbs.
sophisticated. Someone knowledgeable and responsible.
supervisor. Someone who looks over you to make sure you are doing
    all right.
sweet seasoning. A blend of sweet spices.
to taste. To one's own preference; to add flavor.
thicken. To add thickness to sauce.
unconventional. Uncommon; not usual; or not standard.
varieties. Different types.

Special Note: may be hot/spicy.

Types of Pasta

Mentioned in this book's recipes:
  cavatappi
  elbow
  long noodles (packaged Ramen or other long type of noodles)
  pastina (baby stars)
  penne rigate
  rotelle (spirals)
  shells
  thin spaghetti (long)
  ziti rigati

Some other variations:
  angel hair (long)
  bow ties
  egg noodles
  spaghetti (long)
  vermicelli (long)

Note of interest: Some pastas vary in size by number, so the same name can have two or more variations according to size.

Hint: You can sub cavatappi noodles in your homestyle noods with two types of noodles of the approximate same size for a fun variation, especially if your low on one type of noodle. Make sure they are approximately the same size; otherwise, you will not be able to heat them correctly together.

Note: If you are making a cold pasta salad, rinse noodles with cold water and let cool, then add ingredients (cold)—seasoning, olive oil or dressing, blanched peppers, cherry tomatoes, broccoli, etc.—and refrigerate dish.

You can also rinse the noodles, if you feel the need, with any of the recipes above and then add a bit more water with seasoning and other ingredients for sauce. However, with this method, the water should already have boiled into your noodles to make them plump. You may not have access to water in your room if you have to share a community bathroom, and you won't want to waste your bottled water. Most pastas are cleaned before packaging as required by the FDA, and boiling will sanitize your pasta as it cooks, so it may not be necessary with this method.

Appendix A

Cooking Meats without a Stove Top

Off to college, you may not always have access to the community stove in your dormitory if there is one. You may be able to bring in a George Foreman or other small grilling appliance, or you may be lucky enough to have a toaster oven that may allow you to cook some meats if you are careful. There is a way to cook meat in the microwave, which will be explained below. However, there are dangers in cooking meats especially in your dorm room: cross contamination, salmonella, and other bacteria that can cause illness when handling meat improperly. The recipes in this book do not require meat, although some recipes note that you can add precooked meat (already cooked) to enhance your dish. Maybe you went out with friends and have a portion of your meal left over from a restaurant, you have something in your mini fridge from the school cafeteria or outing, or a parent or friend sent you something from home. Those could easily be heated separately and added to your dish.

If, however, you do choose to try cooking meat you may have bought at the local grocery store, this information may come in handy. Of course, your appliance may give you instructions, if you're lucky to have brought or be able to use a roommate's grill. Toaster ovens may be dangerous with meats, but you may be able to cook meat with the right toaster oven pan, as long as you clean up after and keep your station clean.

Any easy way to cook meat in the microwave is the boiling method. However, you may have to cut your meat, and that is when you will have to be careful of bacteria. You will need a clean space, cutting board, and trash can with waste bag and to be able to wipe up and clean your board and utensils immediately ASAP.

Chicken can be cut into small cubes or thin slices and covered with water and brought to a boil, just as your noodles. However, it is advised to cook meat separately beforehand and then add it to your dish or plate after and add your pasta to your meat. You can also boil your chicken and then brown in the toaster oven if available. You may be able to brown in the microwave using a microwave safe glass container if you add butter, but to get the desired grill effect, it is better to use a foreman or similar appliance or toaster oven with pan, just be sure to watch because grease fires can occur and is why some dorms may not allow them.

Similar to the above method, small cuts of steak may also be prepared this way. Cutting your meats beforehand will ensure it being thoroughly cooked all the way through. Otherwise, a small cut that is thick may require a thermometer to ensure proper temperature. Thin slices are recommended for this type of cooking.

Ground meats are commonly defrosted in the microwave. You can defrost your meat fully, add water and seasonings, and continue cooking until browned. It would best to try only a small portion and not a full package to ensure it to be fully cooked. Any remaining portion must be wrapped properly (Ziploc or Saran wrap) and refrigerated (stored on the bottom shelf of the mini fridge to avoid drippage and contamination of other items). Try not to drip any juices from the package or wipe up immediately if this happens. You don't want to be responsible for you or your roommate getting sick.

It is probably better to just buy precooked meats from your cafeteria or nearby restaurant to add a protein to your dish, but just in case you are daring and knowledgeable enough to try, these methods may be helpful.

Lunch meats can also be seasoned lightly and heated to create a dinner version as well, Canadian lunch meat style or sliced into strips, flat cubes, or minced.

Bacon can be laid out in strips on paper or regular plate with lg or 2 to 3 sheets of paper towels below and covering the bacon to avoid grease spatter and cooked in the microwave. (Note: try to space bacon so that edges don't touch.) Other instructions may be on package, such as times.

Be careful of grease fire if cooking in toaster oven. You will not be able to use paper towels in toaster oven; watch carefully and flip once browned on one side. (Use clean pan without holes; usually this pan comes with toaster oven in box.) Other toaster oven pans may be bought separately.

Important: Always wash your hands after handling raw meat. Wash your hands, utensils, and cutting board immediately after use. To avoid spread of harmful bacteria and germs.

Appendix B

Adding Vegetables to Your Dish

Sometimes, you'll want more than just noodles. Although some sauces will have vegetable flavor, you may want to add the real thing if meat isn't a feasible option at the time or for one's palate. If you have a nearby grocery store, picking up a fresh produce may be convenient, and you can add it to your dish. Other options are frozen or canned vegetables.

As mentioned in a recipe above, you can use the water from the can or frozen vegetables to create an easy way to cook your pasta. Frozen vegetables may require you to heat partially prior, but check your times on the frozen package to be sure. You can also heat each item separately and then add them together with your seasoning to finish the recipe and additional heating time.

Fresh vegetables can be bought precut or you can decide to wash and cut it yourself, provided this is permitted in your dorm; however, this may be unlikely, according to most college dorm policies. If allowable, a small/medium dice or medium julienne would be most fitting for the above single-dish recipes.

The blanching method is briefly mentioned in the pages prior and requires you to sanitize the vegetables, briefly using the boiling method without losing the vegetables' bright color. This method is good especially for cold pasta salads but also if you want the fresh, hearty vegetable flavor with still a bit of crunch atop one of your pastas (best for Sweet Almond Pasta Swirl, just add bright-red and green peppers or carrots and broccoli). You can also cook your vegetables further to soften them, and adding seasoning to them will also brighten your dish in a different way. The vegetable choice is really yours.

Cooking, although easy, fun, and exciting—if you have the time and space as well as creative desire to pursue it—can also be difficult and challenging. It is especially challenging if you are confined to a dorm space, the common living style for most students.

The styles of cooking can almost be seen as a vegetable. Like a vegetable starts from a seed, it grows with time and effort into a crisp, hearty vegetable that can then be used in various ways to an elaborate amount of dishes, still whole as the hearty vegetable that it is and tasty. It then can be used with so many styles and ways that it is almost unlimited.

Appendix C

Important Measurements and Conversions

1 oz = standard sauce on side
1 cup = 8 oz
equation: 4 oz = ?
3 tsp = 1 tbsp
1/8 to 1/4 tsp S&P or standard to-go packet
1 tbsp butter = 1 notch
1 individual package of almonds = 43 g (1.5 oz)
1 bottle of water = 8 oz (Cover noodles only to cover them; you can add water if needed for sauce.)
8 in diameter (d) = microwave-safe bowl

The amount of noodles should be enough for single serving—about 1/8 of a standard box/package of noodles.

Coming Soon

Other culinary recipe books by culinary artist creative developer Christine N. McGivern: *Easy and Fun Kid/Baby Meals and Snacks*

Easy Dorm Recipes 2, Christine N. McGivern Culinary Artist Creative Developer

Sweet and Spicy Dorito Crunch Smart Pop Remix

Sweet and Spicy Doritos, Smartfood white cheddar Popcorn, Cinnamon Toast Crunch Remix.

Easy and Fun Kids Recipes, by Christine N. McGivern Culinary Artist Creative Developer

Fun Summer Snack, Pirate Booty Mix

Pirate Booty, Pretzels, Goldfish, Cinnamon Toast Crunch.

Culinary Artist Creative Developer Christine N. McGivern

About the Author

Christine McGivern, although she did not go away to a college to live the normal college dorm life, she somewhat ran into circumstances that required her to manage, as someone might have to, in that style of living.

In her own bedroom on Long Island, New York, she commuted from and through home, local schools, including that of culinary school, and the many jobs that she worked to support herself. Finding very little time to get a meal in and have access to her preferred style of cooking, in a regular kitchen, even in her own home, she came up with a fast and convenient method to manage.

She has, in her travels, visited the college dorm life and found others to be in a similar situation, thus was her reasoning for wanting to pass her knowledge, to help the later generation get by with this book, to become a "ghetto superstar" and survive a challenging life.